ANGEL
VOICES

❖

The Advanced Handbook
for Aspiring Angels

❖

BY KAREN GOLDMAN

Illustrations by Anthony D'Agostino

❖

SIMON & SCHUSTER
NEW YORK • London • Toronto • Sydney • Tokyo • Singapore

SIMON & SCHUSTER
Rockefeller Center
1230 Avenue of the Americas
New York, New York 10020

SIMON & SCHUSTER and colophon are registered trademarks of Simon & Schuster Inc.

Designed by Charles Kreloff
Manufactured in the United States of America

1   3   5   7   9   10   8   6   4   2

Library of Congress Cataloging-in-Publication Data is available.

ISBN: 0-671-88079-9

DEDICATION

This book was written as a special tribute to the dignity and power of that most precious part of all beings, which is an "angel." To all angels everywhere and wherever we may find them. To all the angels still to come. To saints and sages in ages past and ages yet to be. To every soul in every stage of progress. To the people we have loved and who've loved us, here and in the Hereafter, who've made our lives a little sweeter, a little brighter, warmer, lighter, happier, because they exist. To the angelic part of all Humanity that is forever beautiful and loving and never wavers through seasons, circumstances, and even centuries come and go. Especially, to the aspiring angel inside ourselves that we can never love nor appreciate too much, because in truth it is who and what we are and, at its Source, is Divine . . . to the heart of Mankind and the spirit of Love.

ACKNOWLEDGMENTS

I'd like to thank the Sedona Institute in Phoenix, Arizona, for giving me my all-time favorite, simple, totally pure, no-nonsense, powerful, utterly profound way to happiness, abundance, and love. It's the best I have ever found for freeing my own "inner angel" in all ways, at my own pace, by a unique method of releasing unwanted negativity of all kinds—the use of which has changed my life with miraculous results.

❖

I'd also like to thank Self-Realization Fellowship for tremendous inner support and many miracles of transcendent love which never fail to keep me on my toes and sometimes slightly off the ground.

❖

Thanks also goes to Francis Delia for his friendship, humor, care, and expert assistance which really helped get this ball rolling; Patty Leasure for lots of patience, expertise, creativity, and hard work; Eric Weis, M.F.C.C., my friend and supporter; Tony D'Agostino for yet another round of light-filled, heaven-inspired angel paintings; Al Lowman, my angel agent, the best there is; and all my true Friends . . . those visible and those not.

Contents

❖

❖

Foreword: Confessions of an Aspiring Angel

Dear Reader: I have always had an interest in things that are invisible. It was to the invisible that I have looked for answers. My father's death proved to me at an early age with unquestionable finality that what we see is not so important. It is the invisible that has total power over us, the invisible that is in charge.

The Angel Book and *Angel Voices* have been great gifts for me to unify my thinking and my heart. They came to me from a very special, precious place because I needed to heal what was there so I could be whole again. It is an honor and privilege to share with you what I feel the angels have given to me.

Many tears and joys have surged through me in opening myself to these thoughts and feelings and to angels. The angel notes in these pages begin to answer some questions I have been asking all my life. But in any book as in life, or in poetry, the greater message is always found between the lines.

Therefore I do not try to define the word *angel* too closely. I have coined the words "inner angel" and "angelself" and "the angel within" to describe that part of us which is like an angel. I think definitions sometimes get in the way in these matters. Often, the important things have little to do with the mind, but a lot to do with the heart and spirit. You may take this message as metaphor or truth, whichever you choose. But if you listen well, you may know that there is much to be learned about ourselves, even in fairy tales. . . .

INTRODUCTION

A Time for Angels

Angel Voices is about the layers of our Being . . . about light and dark, good and bad, Heaven and Hell, earth and sky, happiness and sorrow. This book is about the place where all opposites meet . . . the horizons of the soul and what lies beyond them. It is about where the angels *really* live.

Angels teach us about total freedom and the places there are no maps to get to, the experiences outside the heaviness of ordinary thinking, about the flow and rhythm of love which takes us there, and how it is we ever do find them, and why we don't live there always.

Angels bring messages not for the intellect, but for the soul. This is not text, but notes, like music; not to be learned, but listened to; not to be understood, but felt. Understanding angels is an exercise in intuition. Intuition is an exercise, not in "figuring out," but in "knowing."

As you read this book, remember, language is not perfect. It is only a shadow of what we experience. We must move beyond all shadows and listen like angels—through the skin and dreams and heart. Angels do not explain themselves. To be understood, they must be experienced through courage, determination, and the desire to be happy.

❖

Angel Voices addresses the inner person. It examines the road to the goal in consciousness, which has no road. It is about the goal of Being. This is a directional book like *The Angel Book*— for those already ascending into the light and seeking its source.

❖

The angels wish that the reader will soon set upon a path that takes him to the end of all angel-journeys where there are no longer problems, solutions, or goals, but a place of Greatness beyond definition—a joy-filled harmony where Happiness simply is, eternally, and in all ways there is Peace.

❖

Begin by remembering everything you've ever been told about angels: everything you've thought, your dreams and visions of them. Then listen.

❖

The story begins like this: Once upon a time in your life, there was a little angel whose name was your name, whose face was your face, whose heart belonged to you and to every other, too. . . .

As an angel you will know the stuff dreams are made of— they are made of you. . . .

❖

The angels will help you retrace your steps to Heaven, lighting new paths and closing the distance between that which you are and that which you can be.

❖

The time is ripe to talk about angels for what they are. The heavens are all set. The journey begins. A new day is dawning, and there are angels all around us everywhere.

❖

The Great One made angels as a bridge. We can all be bridges.
We have all known angels. And we are all going Home.

❖

Settle back. Begin the way you did on the day you were born—
open. You have the rest of your life to do whatever you wish.
But there is only now to become an "angel."

❖

Breathe deep. . . . Be still. . . . You can hear the angels
talking. . . .

Angel Voices

We can hear our angels' voices through the window of our imaginations and the open door of our hearts.

❖

The voices of angels come to us in many ways—they come on quality wings of tenderness and healing; beauty and rekindled wonder; wings of healing and hope; comfort and kindness. Their verdict is always innocent, their sentence always love.

❖

Angels are found hovering in the pauses and spaces between our imaginings; between our feelings and thoughts and perceptions; whenever we forget ourselves for a moment and do not hold on too tightly to our pain. The angels need room to enter in and, likewise, to come out.

❖

The voices of goodness, reason, and hope are within us. And the more we listen, the more we will hear the voices of heavenly angels pressing their lips to our inner minds, speaking poetry in the fine air of our imaginations.

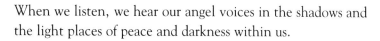

❖

When we listen, we hear our angel voices in the shadows and the light places of peace and darkness within us.

❖

❖The voices of our angels bear witness to the triumphs of Spirit.

❖

❖As we open to our angels, we become healed by our own surrender; changed by what we receive; happy and whole by what we remember.

❖

❖Angels answer questions emanating from the depths of our souls, even those hidden inside us yet to be asked.

❖

❖The teachings of angels are precious gifts to be gleaned from the caves of undisturbed silence deep within ourselves like crystals ever growing because they are alive.

❖

Heaven never wishes to punish, but only to heal; never to accuse, but to vanquish all misery. It is a lean time on earth for Truth, and her flags must wave and her sails must fill again with the winds of kindness and well-being. A pleasant breeze must blow in places where coldness has found shelter too long . . . in the hearts of people.

❖

The tenderest dealings with Spirit will begin as soon as we
emerge into the light of our own souls because this is where we
will find our deeper passion, our comfort, and the greater heart
of our love.

❖

When we listen, angels teach us about knowledge and
ignorance and what separates them . . . the dance of life and
the stillness of Being . . . our hearts and our hates, our freedom
and our smallness . . . the end of all journeys and the
beginning of one true journey. . . . They teach about walls,
and what lies beyond them . . . the known and the unknown
. . . common sense and the uncommon senses; about what is
pure and what is not . . . what cries and what never will.

❖

The angel within must be awakened to view the spectacle of
Paradise that exists beyond our senses; to hear the caring,
nurturing voice of Truth speaking flawlessly and continuously in
the inner chambers of consciousness; and to feel the comforting
breeze of Peace blowing soothingly over the soul.

❖

Our angel voices come from a place where we do not think,
from a quietness inside us and all around us, from a pristine
place where Love is cherished above all else, where decency

drives home the arrows of our souls like Cupid killing all
pretense and freeing everything innocent and perfect within us.

❖

When seeking Truth, look close to Home; for if Truth only
existed in faraway places, where would we find hope and what
good could angels really be?

❖

Whether a holy winged apparition beams silent truths to us in
our own room; or a messenger appears in our dreams in the
night; or if Heaven speaks through the silences in our soul,
through the lips of a stranger, through friends and children; or
the kingdom of paradise within us reverberates with love in our
meditations; or our intuition speaks softly in words, feelings,
and a sense of things to come . . . these are the voices of our
angels, gifts that uplift, console, reward, and caress our very
being, leading us always toward our freedom.

❖

The angels are emissaries from above for all those who have
been told that what they want can only be found in fairy tales
—that they are dreamers and should come down out of the
clouds and live in the real world.

❖

The angels whirl and dance together through all the lands of time and place, pulling and weaving threads of light in their movements toward the One; grabbing open hands, encircling kneeling prayers, lifting everyone with voice and eye and heart, uplifted to the dance and to the magic of everything good.

❖

❖The angels are not hiding from us. We are hiding from them.

❖

Come to the island of angelic thoughts within you. Breathe. Let yourself be surrounded by angels. Think of it as a journey into yourself, where you can dance with birds and find the volcano of Truth within you and see the clouds of love wrapped around the mountain of your spirit.

❖

Be aware of the lightning, the flowers and the rainbows, the volcanoes, the light, and the storms within on the island of yourself in the ocean of God.

PART ONE

—

TEACHINGS

—

ANGEL SONGS

I

Horizons

Love is that little strip of light we can still see on the Horizon when the world is very dark.

Angels have no beginning and no end. They exist in this moment, and not in memories, or projections. To find angels, we must look into the core of our Being.

❖

For this is angel territory. We exist on the border between the known and the unknown, the light and the dark. We are human BEINGS: creatures of two worlds—a part of everything we see, and a part of everything unseeable.

❖

The Truth must be discovered between the edges of our inner and outer vision, where the invisible meets the material. We must go through the door of our own intuition, through the window of our love, through the skylight of our happiness to find Truth. It waits for us.

Angels linger around the edges of our consciousness. Angels are always available . . . always here with us . . . always in the Now.

❖

When we let the angels keep our tummies full and our feet warm for inner traveling, we never worry anymore about our futures or our pasts, and we are not afraid to move.

❖

We know the light will never leave us because it can't. We can only shut it out of sight until we open our hearts and look again.

❖

We are beings of earth and Heaven. We are rich and we are poor, grand and meek like the sea and the simple sand. On the Horizon where Infinity meets the humble inside us, the angels like to visit.

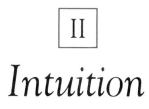

II

Intuition

---

*Within the mind of God is the heart of all things. Within the heart of
a human being is the clear mind of God.*

Intuition is not just a mysterious sixth sense, it *is* sense.
Intuition means knowing what we know. Not hiding from our
knowing, but embracing it and trusting our invisible selves.

❖

Intuition is not a fancy, showy, outrageous ability. It is a
gentle, natural listening and hearing, feeling and sensing,
asking and knowing. Intuition is the water in the lake of our
Consciousness. We are always welcome to sail.

❖

When we feel compassion, we take the shape of that which we
see, we understand a thing; we can hold its form, feel its
weight, see its color, hear its sound, know its mind, grow
within its heart. We think as poets, and understand as angels.

❖

When we see the world through the eyes of children, we are seeing correctly. Their intuition is perfect. There is no prejudice or doubt in their vision. Children understand life, unlearned and naive though they be.

❖

When you can stand in your own humanity like a child, the answers you seek are near.

❖

When we ascend into wonder, we call forth that part of ourselves beyond our knowing where all things are miraculous, and though we do not interpret, we understand.

❖

Truth surpasses our limited understanding. Therefore, aspiring angels seek answers beyond the mind.

❖

Only the awakened among us are not dreaming and have their angels with them always in view.

❖

As mortals we are coursing down a highway which has no name; whose direction we don't know; the Source and End of which remains a mystery. At best, the light of our intuition must be on.

We are living not to accumulate memories, but to awaken while living; to experience ourselves outside Time, where we are complete, ageless, with all potential. To know our greater Being enjoined with the All. To experience one life, one truth, one love, and to identify this, finally, as the center of ourselves.

❖

When one does not lie about who he is, he can never be fooled by others. The honest man sees only other angels and bad actors pretending they are not themselves.

❖

Often, we barely speak to each other. The rest of nature communicates with itself far more fluently than we. When we close our eyes on most nights, have we even spoken intimately with ourselves?

❖

Angels talk to those who are listening like children, without judgment, full of innocence. Our intuition is our natural communication with our greater Souls.

❖

When all you know is small and all you don't know great, rest assured there is Greatness approaching.

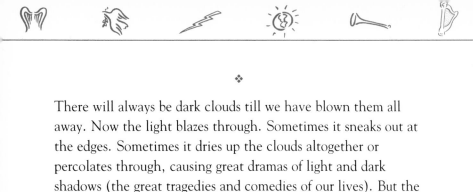

❖

There will always be dark clouds till we have blown them all away. Now the light blazes through. Sometimes it sneaks out at the edges. Sometimes it dries up the clouds altogether or percolates through, causing great dramas of light and dark shadows (the great tragedies and comedies of our lives). But the light is always there. It is never nighttime in the soul.

III

The Unknown

---

*The Unknown is the place from which all realities spring. It is a pure
place without expectation or judgment or lack.*

The Unknown is the factory of the universe. Not a noisy
bustling dangerous place, but quiet and peaceful and inviting
like real magic always is.

❖

Our lives are governed by things invisible. We are blind, in
essence. Yet when we look inward toward Love, out of which
all positive passions, ideas, and energies come, we begin to see
. . . new things . . . clear things . . . the machinery of
creation . . . the Being beyond all beings . . . the purity of life
out of which all living things emerge. These are the realms of
genius, of inspiration, and of angels—the place to which pure-
minded people, angels, and children look and find beauty and
all that which to most remains a secret.

❖

31

When the Soul doors are open to experience angels, reality becomes transparent. You can see the workings of creation.

❖

With the help of our angels, we find answers to questions our minds can never manage to ask.

❖

We can all advance ourselves beyond the scope of things we know into the gleaming, glowing, radiant Unknown . . . where tension is released because it does not belong . . . where the angels of mercy grant our wishes, heal our pretendings, and stroke our simple souls. Our vanity will fall from us like dry leaves from a tree.

❖

What is Spirit? It is what cannot be labeled or pronounced or captured, yet exists. Like the angels, we are also of Spirit.

❖

As mortals we fear falling, though we are traveling uncontrollably and uncharted through space. We hope no one will notice or realize that we do not belong, so we do not reveal to one another very often, nor even to ourselves, how very frightened we are to be here—to land.

❖

We resist being mortal, feeling the weight of our bones and the tenuousness of our flesh. But even more, perhaps, we are terrified by the thrill of our own weightlessness and our gracefulness when we let go, our ability to soar in places we only like to dream of, and of landing lightly on our own two feet like angels right in the midst of our own lives. For we are human and are accustomed to fear.

❖

As angels, we have no fear. No dangers of earth can rise against us. We are creatures of magic and love, unstoppable and invincible—and nature knows it. Yet this is our birthright and our calling. We can exist beyond the trap of our mortality. We are meant to transcend our skin and feel the fires of Heaven glowing within us; to know the healing waters of joy and compassion that flow simultaneously through everything known and unknown, cleansing everything. To witness the miracles of creation and dissolution, exploding in every atom of space all around us . . . to produce miracles of sanity and hold jewels of freedom in our hands. As angels we can know intimately that which was never born and will never die as the foundation of all things known.

❖

As angels, we must be willing to face the Unknown to find our Freedom.

❖

The path to the Unknown is exquisitely beautiful. It is a journey which does not feed us but releases our bodies so we do not need food. It does not comfort us—but lets us break and then it says, "There, you are better off now because you are open."

❖

As mortals, we have forgotten which part is the dream being dreamed and which is us. We have temporarily given ourselves into the hands of this dreaming and have forgotten to wake up. The angels are waiting for us to awaken ourselves.

❖

When we are trapped in a dark room, we want to know *where* the door is. It is not *what* a door is. It's our way out, into the light. The light cannot be known in our limited way of understanding but must be opened to and received innocently, like angels.

IV

Journeys

Our goal must be to find the road to our angels, all angels within ourselves.

The journey of a thousand miles begins with one step. The journey to the soul begins with one heart.

❖

The worlds of the spiritualist and materialist are the same, but the materialist has forgotten he is Spirit, and sees only the obvious—the outer shells of things. He uses only his physical eyes.

❖

An aspiring angel looks beyond his five senses to where meaning lives, to where love flourishes and the heart itself blooms. He lives identified not with the physical, but with the spiritual. His atmosphere is joy; the water he drinks is beauty; his home has walls of love; the sun that shines on him is wisdom; his work is kindness; his food is God. His hobby is devotion; his charity is inspiring others. When he awakens in the mornings he bathes his insides as well as out. His vacations are journeys into Peace.

Your feet only help you travel through the world. It is your Spirit that reaches into the Heaven beyond your thoughts; that carries you beyond the mundane cares of this world; that allows the best in you to take wing.

There are few mistakes that one can make when one is firmly on the path to the Divine. The main mistake then, is getting off.

On the journey Home . . .
. . . There are really no tricks or poor teachers—for even in betrayal and failure do we learn that on which we *can* depend.
. . . There are no wrong ways or paths of no return—for all roads, even crooked and broken, eventually lead again to the Supreme One from whence they have also begun.
. . . There are no real enemies, obstacles, or dangers, for the body is no judge of real Greatness nor of Love.
. . . There are no opponents, for no one can conquer God nor His chosen.
. . . There are no pitfalls, for the heart that wants Freedom will

endure and find the road that rises above any challenge.

. . . And there are no fortunes to be won or lost, save the one for which there is no owner, trustee, nor guardian.

. . . And there are no false finishes, losers, or winners, because in the end, all paths meet where everything exists as One.

. . . Then, there are no outsiders, no angels, sinners, or saints, and God's almighty hand applauds . . .

❖

❖Peace is the road which leads the angels Home.

V

Freedom

Being an angel is not a balancing act, but one of ultimate, steadfast purpose connected to the greatest force in the universe—the force of Freedom.

We are all searching for freedom in our different ways . . . seeking Heaven . . . aspiring to something beyond our reality which we cannot see . . . something invisible . . . something wonderful. It peeks at us from the objects of our desires. It winks at us from the night sky. Often it taps us on the shoulder in our travels and then runs away. It is our Soul . . . our Self . . . our Heaven—the Truth. We try ever to discover it. We long for it. It is seeking us, too. The separation we feel hurts. We must remember there are angels everywhere to direct us back. And as angels we may seek Freedom ourselves, and find it, for always.

❖

In Spirit are all the expansive feelings—love, happiness, joy, ecstasy. To go toward Heaven is to expand. Not to limit, but to become Free.

An angel does not shrink to fit small situations but transcends the walls of circumstance to accommodate his freedom and the freedom of others.

Everyone is an aspiring angel. Everyone is born with the desire to fly. Unfortunately, sometimes the quickest way to Heaven is to finish a long fall. There are those on the way up and those on their way down, excluding our little stumbles. When people are eager to go in the wrong direction, it is often because their angels know, somehow, that once they finally hit bottom (though it may be with a terrible bump), the time will be shorter before they can rise up again and seek their freedom.

We can't deny that we have a past, but we can see *through* it with beams of angel-light to dissolve its pain.

There is no end of grief to the grieving; no safety to the fearful; no comfort to the miserable; no peace to the agitated; and no love to the lonely. But to one who lives in God's presence,

there is no Hell; to one who hears the music of Creation there is no discord; to one who quenches his Being in the rivers of Heavenly joy, there is no thirst for pleasure nor emptiness to fill; to one who walks holding God's gentle hand, there are no more wars. And there is no more darkness to the one lit within.

❖

Whatever we have not let go of has hold of us. Whatever we believe ourselves to be owns us. Whatever we have need of runs us, but as angels, we are free.

❖

❖Freedom attaches to no one and to nothing, except Spirit.

❖Your inner angel is moved by the freedom and simplicities of Being. It has very simple tastes.

❖

Even success is only a gimmick to teach our souls about freedom and to help us see our limitlessness. When we say we're limited it's like roping off a part of the ocean of our Being, saying, "This is mine." If we take down the ropes of our self-imposed boundaries and definitions, we let in all the abundance that we are.

❖

There are many natural wonders in the world, but there is really only one flawless experience; and that is of our own flawlessness, our own nature, beyond form, identity, or cause. The degree to which we know our entirely free, indescribable angel-nature is the degree to which we will be angels on earth —human angels.

❖

As free Beings we profess no plan for our own salvation. We do not struggle here but reach effortlessly beyond the boundaries of ourselves—finding solitude and passion and solutions in the measureless calm emanating everywhere.

❖

We come from freedom . . . we are returning to freedom . . . it is freedom we seek in every act.

❖

We cannot hold Truth in our hand but breathe it in and out, making all the light around us dance, seeing the goodness reflected in the crystal grains of our honesty like diamonds brightening the way for all who seek Heaven.

❖

Free will is a camel that brings the water of hope to the desert of fear.

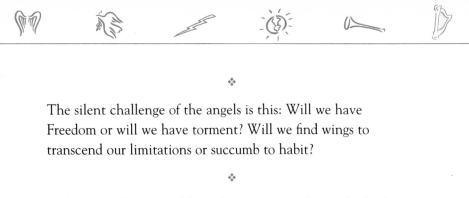

❖

The silent challenge of the angels is this: Will we have Freedom or will we have torment? Will we find wings to transcend our limitations or succumb to habit?

❖

❖The joys of freedom, like a child, come to those who both desire it and let it go.

❖To the angels, the true goal of life is not the end of struggle but the beginning of Freedom.

❖An angel's most precious possession is Freedom.

VI

Home

To angels home is not only where the heart is—but all hearts.

Home is not far away and hard to get to. It is the place underneath your own skin inside your bones, behind every dream and song in your own heart—the place you discover when you are not afraid anymore; where you are always safe and protected; where there is an infinite playground for your enjoyment with no hidden agendas.

❖

Home is a place not of boredom, but of tranquillity—not of blindness, but of clear vision where one can see, without reacting; a land of deep faith and beauty. An inner Heaven where all things bring Peace and all roads lead to Harmony. There is no time there, nor distance to the self, nor any other blockage obstructing the sunshine of Being.

❖

When we are Home there is no distance to the self; no route being followed to the Goal. The traveler has arrived, and with him comes all Creation in his pocket. He does not strive for glory, power, or riches. He has become them; he embodies them. He carries them as effortlessly as the air he breathes.

❖

There is no place on earth more safe and peaceful, alive and replenishing, than the Home within you when you need rest.

❖

Whenever you are tranquil of heart, when you feel as your only need that need to travel deeper into your own soul—you may know you will soon come out the other side. And they will all be waiting—legions of them, armies, cities of angels to take you Home.

❖

Home is a place where the masters walk unimpeded through every trial of life. Here Truth bubbles through the earth, through the atoms of the air, through the trees and plants and people—through the pores and cells of all space—like an ocean pulsing with light. And just beyond it, on the Horizon, we see the calm of Heavenly Peace. It is inside us.

❖

Being Home is knowing the deeper essence of the Truth and then walking with it; not adding or subtracting to suit our purposes, just walking with it, as it is.

❖

The walls of our inner Home can withstand any force and do not buckle or sway when the land shifts. The door is always open to those who seek sanctuary, yet no evil force can penetrate.

❖

In the quiet moments when one knows the true meaning of rest, the angels gather, forcing their way so gently into the pools of our memories and premonitions; shadowboxing for us with our fears; touching our fingers and our toes with breezes of delight and delicate playfulness as if we were babies. They surround our musings like butterflies, waiting to ascend. They capture our attention in sunlight and flickering blades of grass. They hand us our hearts to examine, tenderly wishing us Peace, teaching us to breathe when we have lost our way, calming our essence with the cool mist of clarity, climbing into our souls like true believers, true friends put to the test. They come with happy hearts. Like the faithful called to glory, they sing to our resting souls handing out gifts of inspiration like cherished elders.

❖

❖Home is a tender place where mercy reigns; and like a river quenches our thirst for all things beautiful and holy and free.

❖When there is no violence left in you of any consequence, you will know you have traveled the right road and are close to Home.

❖The wise struggle to be free in life, which always guides them to their own front door.

❖

Truth is a banquet that waits for you. The table is set. The food is warm and delicious. The chairs are comfortable. The service is Divine. No reservations. Open all the time. Come as you are.

❖

Go Home when weary; when the force of your joy drains into the emptiness of unsmiling routines; when life's beauty runs from you like a frightened child.

❖

When we return Home, inside ourselves, all menacing ends. We go to meet our Maker like naughty children trusting we will be forgiven, and we return into our angelselves rocked softly by the wings inside God's own heart.

VII

Windows

When we open our angel windows, we can see Heaven.

Angels are the eyes and ears of the soul, spreading kindness through portals of Wisdom.

❖

We must be attuned to the language of Paradise to hear our angels.

❖

❖Our answers are found in these windows of consciousness through which we may view Eternity and the grandeur of Love.

❖There is a finer realm where angels live which gives the heart its Magic and the world its Art.

❖

When we are wise enough to follow the advice of our angels we don't need to be tough. They come through us like children in a foreign land, like whispers of love in the night.

❖

When we open our angel windows, we cherish being awake over any dream.

❖

❖When we are receptive, we are surrounded by angels predisposing us to Peace. We are wrapped in clouds of gentleness and pure Magic.

❖Before our eyes can open, our hearts must. Before our hearts can open, our souls must.

❖

Angels gently soothe our anxious fears and ease our bad dreams —simply suggesting that we turn on the night-light of happiness to eliminate darkness; that we remember love, which arises into all broken places and mends our shattered lives like new—only so much better with Divine glue that never *ever* comes apart.

❖

The essence of angels is written in the diary of Creation. Along with flowers and oceans and planets, their blueprint is etched in sacred chapters in all our hearts.

We can choose our identity. We can be fighters and sowers of despair or we can be Heaven's very breath filled with the passions of angels; spreading love where there was none, holding candles in our own darkness, flying headlong into the nature of our Being and never looking back.

❖

We can be silent and still again inside like the children we truly are; a mirror of unlimited beauty that is the Spirit of the angels.

❖

The light is always looking at us. Whenever we look back, we see the sparks we call the good times of our lives.

❖

But where is this other realm that we rise into now and then, from where little gifts are dropped and occasionally a miracle descends? It is right here, ever present behind our own perceptions, alive and glowing with promise. And when we turn within to face ourselves, we remember all that we have forgotten while looking the other way. In an instant we remember ourselves as we really are, and we hear the cheerful sounds of the wings of our angels, who bring us our joy like mother birds, thinking nothing of themselves, always busy to nourish us . . . with love.

❖

Before we fit in to this world, we owned the universe . . .
Before we accepted that some things are impossible, we had the
potential for miracles . . . Before we knew what to say, we
could express our true selves . . . Before we knew where we
belonged, we belonged everywhere. . . .

❖

Before our troubles will leave us we must release the shackles on
our souls. We must let loose the heavy latches on the windows
of our inner Beings. We must spy Heaven through the skylight
of our efforts for Freedom, feel the angels reaching down into
our own Consciousness with threads of sanity and goodwill,
honing in on our enterprises with wings of good fortune.

❖

Angels dream beautiful visions for the world with their eyes
open, watching them come true.

❖

If we listen . . . we will hear. If we are quiet, the sound
increases and so does the silence . . . and so do we.

❖

The angels strum their music sweetly through our soul's open
doors, their music leads us, flows through us, and we flow,
too.

VIII

Grace

Angels dance in step to their own rhythms in harmony with the greatest and smallest rhythms of the universe.

Grace keeps Time moving, our bodies breathing, our souls humming. We are all living in a state of grace.

❖

Grace is a treasure, a package of soul flowers received by intuition to be opened delicately and appreciated forever.

❖

Grace is a sweet gift, and when we own it, it illuminates night with bright singing and morning with flight.

❖

The angels know that getting what we want is small compared to knowing what we have.

❖

The angels hold their hands round us like children cupping candles. They protect us gently lest our flame go out when the wind is strong.

❖

Our inner angel is a master of all that is graceful within us— comfortable with the pure strata of Being and the meticulous manifestations of matter alike. As angels, we attract all that is graceful from outside and above because we are truly one with all that is perfect and we mirror it.

❖

Grace can be found by opening the door to our inner angel and harmonizing ourselves with that place. When we are in tune with our shining, graceful, peaceful selves, the universe responds in kind, paving our angel's way through the thick jungles and traffic jams of human existence.

❖

As human beings sometimes we are not very graceful, we hold on at the wrong times, force in the wrong places, push, weigh ourselves down, and crash through our problems. Other times we let go, become open and permeable to force, and are flexible, weightless, and centered. We feel lifted from within. The energy inside us is fine, the air in our minds is clear.

❖

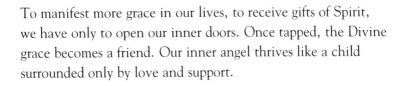

To manifest more grace in our lives, to receive gifts of Spirit, we have only to open our inner doors. Once tapped, the Divine grace becomes a friend. Our inner angel thrives like a child surrounded only by love and support.

❖

Sometimes we are brave souls wandering through the illusions of life, blameless in our ignorance, like children. Sometimes we are timid creatures clinging tight to one another, terrified to look at ourselves in the mirror or gaze into the face of God.

❖

But on gentler days we are soulful, loving friends, treating ourselves to the delights of the Spirit which is in us. We cannot be bought by fear or jealousy, for we are in the indestructible realm of Spirit and for us there is no coming down.

❖

On those days, we are angels capturing the dance of life in the rhythm of our hearts; warming sunnily on the beaches of our better natures; watching the kites of our happiness dance in the winds of grace.

❖

When we are angels, we are unstoppable, never falling but

releasing the fear; never winning but releasing the victory; simply being, acting, giving, and not wanting.

When we are lonely, it is our angels we may turn to to fill our hearts with music and our souls with joy.

❖

When we remove the traffic and noise of our minds and emotions, a graceful ballet of Creation begins. Like beautiful lace or snowflakes, life manifests in pretty patterns, artful designs, varied and infinitely perfect statements of Truth to peruse, enjoy, appreciate, and flow with.

❖

Flocks of birds, schools of fish, mountains of flowers, rays of sunlight—the rest of Creation is not bumping into itself. . . . Why are we?

❖

The angels will help us to see our colors. They are made of light. Their nature, being pure light, includes all colors. We see ourselves, our colors, in them.

❖

As aspiring angels, the deeper reality of Heaven speaks to us even through unfulfilled wishes, broken promises and dreams, and empty longings. They hide the answers to Creation behind their masks, and we can take them off one by one and see our angel-selves again and that we are beautiful and have everything we need already. We remember what heavenly purpose we embody and become like angels mounted inside the cloak of God, listening and offering our selves, accepting His protection and grace, and enjoying the ride.

❖

As mortals we are caught in the branches of our own reasonings, unable to fly, waiting for the little bird of God's grace to alight upon our arm, chirp wisdom in our confused ears, and set us free. As angels, though, we can step bravely out into the unknown to find our freedom and risk the fall in order to fly; risk not knowing in order to know; risk not being noticed in order to find ourselves, at last; risk putting our hearts out on the line for each other and ourselves to discover the real love that fills the air all around us; risk letting go of our petty hates to bask in the good feeling and Peace that is our birthright and our nature and the passion of everyone. Then, grace comes to us like a little bird and never leaves us, filling our lives with music and miracles, poetry and love.

❖Becoming an angel is not a matter of fitting in, but of coming out of oneself into Life.

❖Call upon your angels. Make friends. Keep the door open and be graced.

❖Ask for grace and then accept it when it comes.

❖In our harmlessness, we will find our power; in humility, our strength; in kindness, belonging; and in our tenderness, grace.

PART TWO

—

THE DARKNESS

—

ANGEL WHISPERS

IX

Shadows

The moon comes out when we remember to breathe in our darkness and open our eyes.

An angel's intention is so pure in nature, he casts no shadow upon the world . . . and therefore, none of the world's shadows can fool him. Like angels, we can release our fears and hold on to our innocence.

❖

We alone cast the shadows in our lives. Wherever there is darkness within us it is because we are in the way.

❖

When we come out of the shadows, our spirits rise again, balancing in the freer air, not needing to predict our futures against our pasts, feeling evermore the thrill of weightless surrender to the light.

❖

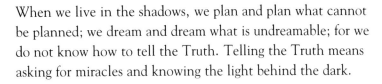

When we live in the shadows, we plan and plan what cannot be planned; we dream and dream what is undreamable; for we do not know how to tell the Truth. Telling the Truth means asking for miracles and knowing the light behind the dark.

❖

When we forget to be angels we fall from grace and nowhere do we see a friend or a familiar face.

❖

As angels we may well ask: "Is it really all right to fly while all the world is crashing? Can we really swim while all the world is sinking? Is it possible to love while all the world is hating?"

❖

As angels we will answer, "Though clouds and death blanket my soul, I will keep shining."

❖

When one wrong thought darkens the way for another Being, our angel light vanishes. But in the sunny reality of Heaven, no shadows or demons lurk; only angels and no darkness exists because there is no one there to cling to it.

❖

As mortals, we hold on to our devils, attracting what we harbor, with nowhere to go to escape ourselves. But we are

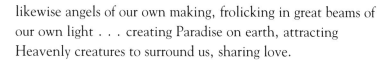

likewise angels of our own making, frolicking in great beams of our own light . . . creating Paradise on earth, attracting Heavenly creatures to surround us, sharing love.

❖

We may travel back and forth between the light and the dark, but we will transcend only through love and finally discover who and what we are, beyond all shadows.

❖

Hiding in the shadow of the mountain is its greatness and character. Hiding in the shadowy awkwardness of our own personalities is an angel who whispers to us the purpose of our lives.

❖

When we are distracted by emotion, negativity, pride, greed, hunger of any kind, our wings will never really open.

❖

Sometimes we become so cut off, so detached, devastated, or depressed that our angel gets locked away in the darkness. We don't see much light, and we don't care. Then, when we choose our freedom again it hurts to see what we have done to ourselves, to this beautiful angel inside us. We weep or we get angry. But that's all right, it's just the clouds parting.

❖

When we see a shadow, do we see the dark or the light around it? Is our life the shadows or the light? It takes dark and light to make a picture, a drama. When we grow tired of dramas and look for the light-source for the show of life, instead of whining for better parts, He rewards us with roles of our choosing—sometimes in front, sometimes behind the scenes. Because then we are Players He can really trust, no longer trying to take credit for every scene. Then we are brilliant knowing we are not working for ourselves, but to express Him.

In the shadows of my darkest dreams I am a hurricane with red-streaked splotches and gold elbows, in a bristling black cape. My hair is spun from iron needles. My teeth grip the night in one embrace. But when I awaken I am an angel. My arms are long. They hold the shadows of the world. And in my hand there is only one raindrop, and I save it for a tear of joy on a dry day.

Old age is a shadow that falls when we have forgotten how to love. (It usually takes many years and plenty of hard work to forget, though a few people master it very young.) As aspiring angels, we never age, nor forget love—nor does it forget us.

The angels do not linger in the shadows. They stand as Reminders just beyond the fingertips of society, culture, personality. Whenever we manage to glance beyond our own shadows in their direction they smile at us—silently singing to our souls those verses that will help us to fly.

X

Separation

As mortals our purpose is hidden from us when we crawl instead of learning to fly.

We hide from our angels behind our masks, pretendings, and outward disguises. We will never find our angels while holding up false pictures of ourselves.

❖

❖We are all living at the scene of the crime of feeling separate.

❖

Separation is a lie. We will never be separate from what we are. You can lose your body, or parts of it, your will to live, you can take a vacation into insanity, break your heart, you can change your name, your identity, your personality can shatter, you can have amnesia, and forget your own face, you can lose everyone you know, your sight, your hearing. You could leave the planet, astral project—but you're not going anywhere.

❖Good and bad, right and wrong, are not answers but labels.
All labels take us not to the Truth, but from it.

❖

❖As angels, one day we will move beyond all separations to
where both light and dark originate—in the land of pure
Being.

❖

There are no borders between earthly and Heavenly worlds,
only those which we draw in our own minds. Every division
makes us suffer, makes us that much smaller. Each line we draw
between our selves and others is our own selfishness trapping
us. If we decide to erase our limitations, we may do so. When
we erase them we will have found our seat in Heaven and will
be joyfully given the keys to all things. It is as simple as that.

❖

❖Because we have forgotten our souls, we wait for happiness.
Because we deny our Truths, we hunger for meaning.
Because we keep silent when we should speak, and speak
when we have nothing to say, we wonder about life and are
puzzled by our purpose.

❖

When someone dies our minds try to swallow the pain but
cannot. There is so much untruth in separation, we cannot

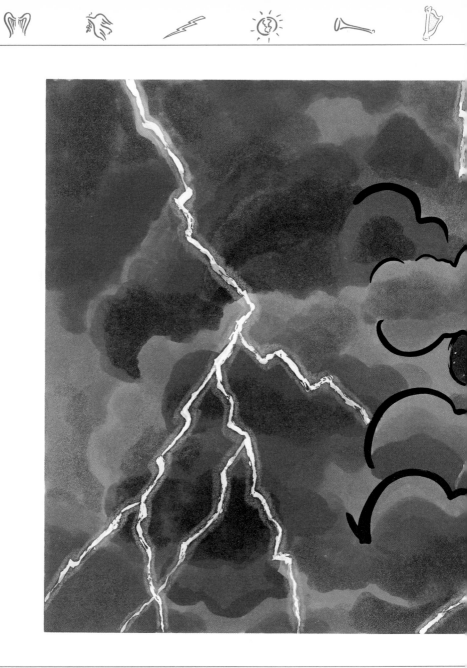

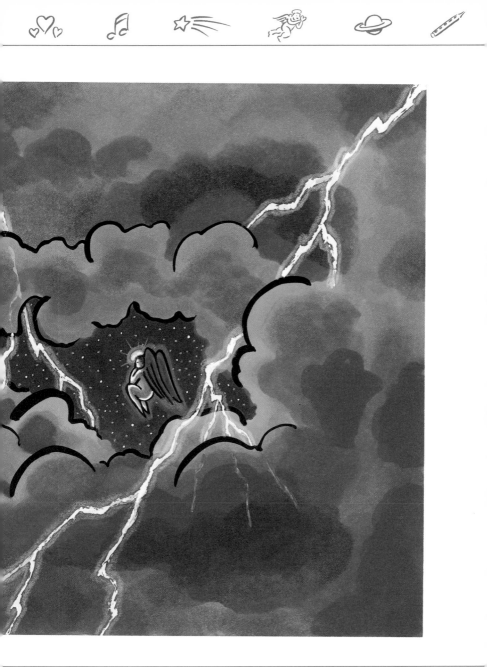

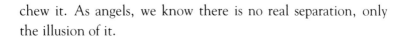

chew it. As angels, we know there is no real separation, only the illusion of it.

❖

The feeling of separateness creates a volcano of pain in every human heart, liable to erupt. To ease the pressure of our lives we must open our hearts to each other and to ourselves, and know that within the love we will discover who and what we are and reclaim our connection to everyone.

74

XI

Nature

Nature is a window to the Soul of God. That is why we are so moved by it. We, too, are windows.

The world is a very green place where happiness blossoms in colored flowers; peace lights the sky; the red earth is rich; and the mountains are brave climbing into the clouds.

❖

Nature hasn't any more instructions than we have. Nature meets life head on and lets its flowers blossom where they may, lets its branches fall where they may. Nature has no regrets, is incapable of lying to itself, holds eternity in each moment gracefully without presumption or consideration, and sways to the rhythm of an eternal and timeless clock.

❖

Nature never needs to escape. She takes comfort and inspiration directly from Life itself and makes us look like busy, complicated creatures who forget we are part of the rest, free to take our nourishment directly, too.

❖

In nature we see what we want to be. Nature shows us our smallness. But our being cries out, "We are unlimited, we are powerful, we are free!"

❖

The birds fly beyond our limitations on fragile feathered wings. The air blows past, moving freely over the earth unaided by feet and bones. The sun shines over our human limits lighting the entire world.

❖

But the light inside us can light the world more brightly than the sun. Our inner wings will take us beyond the sky into unfathomed spheres of beauty.

❖

Within us is the infinite source of energy that conceives each new moment, initiates all motion, all stillness, all peace.

❖

The water and the bumblebee and the moss are all one. Nature does not need to wonder about itself or view itself in parts. Everything works together perfectly.

Everything that is beautiful is also humble. The proud swans must bend their heads to feed. The oak loses its finery for the winter storms. Clouds weep when they become too abundant and grand. So the aspiring angel must bend to that which is greater, yet remain standing and strong through the cold wind of earth life. In nature, we see our reflection and within every image we are reminded to be ever humble.

❖

Nature needs no mind to appreciate itself. Did you ever see anything happier than a flower? A waterfall? Or the lush green moss clinging and snuggling by its bank?

❖

There are no happier places than those to which God has given no cause but to be One.

❖

As an angel, I want to fall into a meadow—and rest in the green enfolding arms of my mother.

XII

Oneness

To the angels, we are all one perfect child with many different faces.

In the world of angels there is no up or down, no time, no names, no movement. All is one complete and perfect experience of love.

❖

Our common perspective on life is filled with conditions, opposites, and distances. To an angel, there is only one condition that applies everywhere, all the time, and within it are the answers to all questions.

❖

To an angel, Oneness is the experience that speaks in all languages, addresses all beings, is available always and everywhere, holds all power, respects and nurtures all hearts, answers all longings, fills all gaps.

❖

The understanding we want is the kind that transcends the separation and fear—the kind of understanding angels have.

❖

There is a way of "knowing" that like an angel defies gravity, defies the intellect, eludes the most scholarly and renowned. It is the experience of unity, by instantaneous knowing, that we are one with all creatures and all Divine Providence.

❖

The greatest message of the angels is that we are not alone but that we are an integral part of One Divine Consciousness with infinite members.

❖

The more we become like angels, the more we give great gifts to the world. And the more we feel unity with every bird, every rock and wild flower, every inch of atmosphere and drop of water, the more alive we are. The more we see and know ourselves everywhere in all people, in all things, the more we admit the presence of Glory in our own humble, sacred hearts.

❖

Only in Oneness do we find true happiness. Its roots are in the unlimited soil of Being.

❖

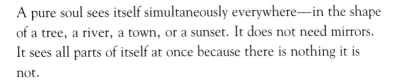

A pure soul sees itself simultaneously everywhere—in the shape of a tree, a river, a town, or a sunset. It does not need mirrors. It sees all parts of itself at once because there is nothing it is not.

❖

If our training has been opposite to these Truths, we must train ourselves to find them, where they are. The answers are not on the shallow, mundane level of our questions. Mundane problems require mundane solutions, but the thrill of life's greatness, of our beauty, and Heaven's magic is not found in the world of separation and fear. It is a little higher up where all is One.

❖

Our souls are united so high above our mortal consciousness that we cannot comprehend it with our minds. In our minds we may be separate, but in our souls—never.

❖

When we devote ourselves to these greater, freer territories of experience, mundane problems and solutions tend to completely take care of themselves, often without needing our attention at all. Things happen for our good—solutions present themselves and Harmony rights "disasters" and "crises" without a thought from us.

❖

We feel gentle and powerful because we are not *alone*.

❖

When we follow the dictates of our angels, we have no enemies; no need to divide, overpower, or conquer. We trust and we wait. We turn the light of our loving attention on our nightmares and wait for that part of ourselves to wake up. It will. It always does—when given a chance.

❖

❖Receptivity is the window to open to the breezes of Oneness.

❖Where pride steps in, the angels step out. Where heaven steps in, the angels dance.

❖In Oneness, there are no "others," only different views of our greater angelselves.

❖Like angels, we soar in unison.

❖

ANGEL ONENESS SONG

"Allow me to be one with that which is behind all Creation. Allow me to be humble to receive that which is grandest and most Divine. Allow my soul to feel the breath of life blowing through

Creation and to know its beauty. Keep me ever mindful of Your love
—its strength to which I owe my strivings; its depth to which I owe
my depth; and Your angels to whom I am beholden for life's many
graces.

❖

"Allow me to know You evermore and lose You never. Let all who
hear Your words make promises to themselves never to turn away
nor break Your sacred trust. For in these times we will see miracles
—and such as men not often dream will be. And never will we be
alone, but often will we remember our angels.

❖

"For Heaven is a greatness from which there is no turning back—a
gladness to which there is no ending. The shorter the distance, the
longer the journey to that which we seek apart from You. And in our
innocence, we see many miracles where miracles do not exist. Yet in
the shining heart, the miracles of love explode daily and are never
noticed from without.

❖

"Where are our angels? Our friends, yet our mystery. Our
protection, yet our hidden guardians. For what do we feel an
emptiness, and from what may we fill our cup?

❖

"In moments of great relief and in moments of great comfort, we break ourselves open to their love and join them. We give up our drama to rest in them. We light for ourselves the match of our intuition. They see it and add a great fire to our little flame. And we see . . . we see.

❖

"We see the folly of our earthbound actions. We are illuminated by the sight of He who sent us here. We see our angels waiting behind all our masks, behind all our devils. They are sweet. They are smiling. They are powerful, but above all, they are there. Then we know we are safe, we are loved, we are not alone, and all is well because of them being there, simply Being."

❖

As mortals, to even speak of being alone makes us shudder, makes us weak to imagine. Or, as angels, we revel in it as solitude and grow infinitely strong. For we are separate and we are One. Each a part of the other, but we can be no one but ourselves. We strive to connect in all manner of friendship. Yet we strive all our lives simply to know who we are.

❖

We must unite to face those trapped outside our hearts. Let everyone come in—and then we will see Peace on Earth when everyone is here, safe together where we belong.

❖

* No *one* can go where God lives . . . only everyone.

* Angels are not elitists. They do not hide from us out of pride, but humility.

* There is no faster way to the Divine than to accept our Oneness.

XIII

Death

To an angel, death is yet another light-filled journey.

The fear of death is a lie that feeds on the unprotected hearts of the shallow and the ignorant, to all of us who cling to mortality for security and to the world for comfort. The angel within must be given permission to stand up and take back the Truth we have given up; to lead us into the silence of Being, where we will remember all that we have forgotten—and be once again the winged immortal children that we are, happy and content on the knee of God.

Everything we are will rejuvenate except the body. When it is broken it will die. When Spirit is broken it will rise again.

❖

Death is only a resting period before the shoots of life sprout up through Consciousness reaching for the sun again.

❖

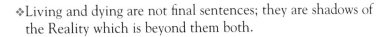

❖Living and dying are not final sentences; they are shadows of the Reality which is beyond them both.

❖The arms of death are gentle and magnificent, ready to express the love we have not yet found in one final embrace.

❖When the time comes, we will leave this earth, but we will never leave our angel-selves.

❖

❖Our souls, like angels, are immortal. If we could only realize this, death would bother us no more.

❖When we fear letting go, we face annihilation. When we rejoice in letting go, we face Heaven.

❖

Fear holds a candle only high enough so we can see death, but not its shape or form or weight. Fear's light spreads darkness, warms no one, grants us no vision. As aspiring angels, we will pull away to walk in our own light, holding candles to a flame high above us for all the world to be illuminated—and then we see things as they really are. And there is light even where the darkness hides when we walk by. One day we will walk by fear, and he will see himself hiding, bitter, visionless. When we ask him to walk with us, he will not. He waits for death . . . not knowing we have conquered it.

❖

❖Angels live beyond living and dying. Their essence is immortal. Their home is all inclusive, beyond the narrow territories of existence we have defined for ourselves.

❖We can die in joy or pain, but not both. Spiritually, we choose our own destiny.

❖Our bodies may be patterned after animals, but our souls . . . like angels.

❖

❖Leaves that fall are saying good-bye. There is no fanfare. It is
the quietest, most graceful thing in the world.

❖

To an angel, death is not an enemy, but a trip to a new country
filled with friends, harmony, and comfort. It is a journey with
wondrous visions that fill one with love.

PART THREE

—

THE LIGHT

—

ANGEL LAUGHTER

XIV

Inspiration

Before we could walk we flew. . . .
Before we could wonder . . . we knew.

*E*verything about angels is rare, uncommonly beautiful, and
yet familiar.

❖

When we are inspired, we are like angels being born, bursting
into view like sunlight into a blackened room.

❖

The senses are befuddled when the soul suddenly "sees" or
"hears" or "feels" an angel. People don't know what they are
experiencing, just something "wonderful," something "special"
—that's all they can say.

❖

When it's time to "turn over a new leaf," we can call for our angels. Is there anything fresher or more inspiring or pure than an angel? We are all budding angels waiting for spring.

❖

We weep and cry out to our brothers when we have nowhere to turn, but we can always call upon our angels when we have lost our light.

❖

When the mind is quiet and at peace, the angel-thoughts can rise to the surface. When the mind is too busy, the angels cannot get through the muck.

❖

When we let form try to define us, we grow useless. When we try to define life too rigidly, existence becomes flat, unattractive, one-dimensional. In our freedom and formlessness is our art.

❖

When the colors change from daylight to night we remember that we too change colors when we move between the light and the dark inside ourselves. And this is the sunrise and sunset of creation, of our souls. It is the drama between our worlds, until one day, when we have had enough of changes and seek to know the source of all the light. Then we become masters of our dramas, and we paint our canvases, our dawns and twilights alike, with skillful hands, like geniuses—like angels.

❖

As a human being, there are anchors tied to my feet, but I don't care, I fly anyway.

❖

Use light to create magic with the Grand Magician. Through His Creation you will find the doors to Him. The doors can be seen everywhere to the discerning eye, felt everywhere to the discerning heart.

❖

As human beings, we have one continuous invitation to open any door to join Him. He is the one true point of Ecstasy . . . the one moment of Harmony . . . the one Happiness inside All . . . happening all the time, whether we are conscious of it or not.

❖

They say, "Do not wait for the music to find you. You must make your own or you will have to depend on the music of others, and that will never be enough to really dance to."

❖

When you listen like an angel, you find all of creation singing
and dancing to the same song. The music glides and ebbs, rises
and falls, dances and plays around and through every atom and
fiber of your Being. That's really listening, and that's music
worth listening to because within it is the soul of real
inspiration.

❖

An angel's inspiration can restore integrity, righteousness, and
humility to a self-obsessed world. All truly great leaders have
unveiled these peaceful angels within themselves and listened
to their songs. Their naturalness and unselfishness free the
angel inside them to perform miracles for the sake of the
innocent, harmless free beings they know others to be. Then,
politics, medicine, science and all religions bow in
acknowledgment.

❖

An Inspiration Story

*Nobody knows where he came from. You can see him moving along
through the orchards in the morning and along the roads in the day,
planting and plucking wisdom like oranges. He carries the sun in a
small basket behind his eyes. He speaks through them on planes of
light. I saw him once. He spoke the sun to me through a screen of*

flowers. He painted indelible words on the canvas of my thoughts. He made magic pictures out of frames of reason. He wove music out of the noises of Being. I was bound for hours in the fine fabric of his aura. But at twilight he faded, and by evening, he was gone.

Whatever an angel has given to you is a gift you are then to give to someone else. And each time the gift changes hands, an angel is born.

XV

Happiness

The angels bloom in the sunshine of our love, dropping petals of happiness to earth.

Whenever we enter the realm of angels, revelations enter the heart, bursting wide its creaky doors, causing mountains of strength to rise where there were none; filling the mind with visions of splendor and bliss that make "reality" take a backseat to joy; vanquishing the ordinary, exuding the miraculous.

❖

❖Real happiness is not an altered state, but a natural one.

❖Happiness is a mirror that reflects only our true self.

❖All the unripe fruit of intellect cannot give us one drop of happiness.

❖Happiness doesn't have to be learned, but arrived at by unlearning our unhappiness.

❖

Don't deny your reality in favor of someone else's. Transform your own by letting go.

❖

You want happiness. That is not a wild dream. Let the angels guide you. Have the riches that will never rust. Be free.

❖

❖ We don't have to be trained into perfection, but untrained.

XVI

Creation

Angels are not dreamers—they are what make dreams come true.

The angels lived before dark was not light, when Time was still and the world not even dreamed; before music, before names, before order or things; when there was absolute Peace of Being and no other.

As mortals, we have tried to live in worlds of our own design, pulling many thoughts and moods around ourselves for comfort. Through the centuries and ages and eons with every comfort we cloak ourselves in, we become further from the One; layer upon layer, further and further, until finally, all that's left to remind us is a memory of the One, a feeling way down underneath, and bits of light peeking out now and then through one another's eyes.

❖

Today, there are those among us who consciously seek our Origin. We search proudly, fearlessly for the road Home, in spite of all the unenlightened attempts to stop us (even the unenlightened within ourselves). All existence then is a journey—not aimless, not outward, but back Home. And those who went before us turn and stop to help, and those behind reach for us and seek our Wisdom. This is where angels come in.

❖

For aspiring angels the deeper reality of Heaven speaks even through our unfulfilled wishes, broken promises, dreams, and empty longings, which hide the answers to Creation behind their masks. As angels, we can take these off one by one and see the beauty and Magic in Creation.

❖

The aspiring angel knows what Power is running the world and propelling its action. We seek that Power, not to harness it for our own ends, but to identify the Soul of all creation as a part of our own soul.

XVII

Poetry and Art

Artists are aspiring angels who give us a peek at God through the open door of their lucid hearts and minds.

Poetry and Art magnify the soul, pulling it into realms unattended for ages, clearing a path through the debris of restlessness and shaking loose the fears that cling to our essence, shouting to our sleeping souls in words of Truth, color and form, shaking us awake, setting us apart from the usual, letting us greet our selves again with cleaner hands and faces, in a new moment of Promise.

❖

Art exposes the angels' movements and holds back nothing, shooting brilliance from soul to soul . . . sending inspiration like angels dancing through the veins . . . borrowing happiness from Everywhere . . . pinpointing Truth incessantly . . . delivering it to our tired, hungry hearts, our waiting thirsty souls . . . restoring our lost beatific vision in perfect bursts of clarity . . . reminding us that there are many, many colors to Heavenly Magic and many artists, but only one Divine brush.

❖

The tender symphonies of color and sound in nature elude our recordings until we throw open the doors and windows of our souls and unite in the joy of the infinite Art, the singing and playing and painting with the Supreme Artist. Only then are we allowed to hold the brush or the pen and even sign our own names.

Creativity is Spirit, leaping into Love, dancing in Truth, plunging into Beauty, by whatever means possible.

❖

The life of an angel is like Poetry. It is Rareness. It is Beauty. It is Happiness. It is Truth. It is Wonder—that which only silence can write about.

❖

Real Poetry ascends through the light and dark delirium of our average lives, past the dilemma of our consciences, to the bright strata where the angels dwell. It assigns us to ourselves for reinventing, colorfully, shamelessly, holding our hand in contemplation, keeping one foot always in the light-filled doorway of God.

❖

When we are not afraid of dying to the intense beauty of reality, we become Divine Artists.

❖

In every act of genius is an element that leads to infinity. The mind cannot follow and steps aside. But the soul rejoices anyway. Only angels voyage to where there are no limitations —Heaven, reflecting that within us which is infinite.

Poetry falls from the sky on a quiet night like this. Anyone can catch it in their hair if they leave their imaginations open.

Angels write and paint into the bare walls of Creation, carving pictures in unseen souls; not dreaming, but digging out the Truth in hard places.

Poetry, like Love, is a charm in the hands of a child. It is a shiny thing glistening in our eye, making us forget who we are so that we can remember something better.

❖ Where Truth and Beauty meet, the angels sing and dance in the splendor of Divine Love.

❖ The Artist is more valuable than his art.

XVIII

Miracles

It doesn't take a lot to make a miracle. It only takes an angel.

Like mothers aware of a child's every blink and nod, angels are a part of the invisible realm where everything comes from, where all miracles are conceived and hope blooms like a thousand-petaled flower, calling us only with her fragrance.

❖

Some plants grow quickly, some slowly, but the real miracle is that they grow. Within our growing is a miracle, too.

❖

When we are "open" to angels, all good things come to us. Whenever you open the door to Life your angel comes out of hiding whether you are aware of it or not, and the universe automatically gives it the best of what it's got. When nothing stands in the way between your angel and the object of your desire, it magically comes to you.

❖

Our destinies cannot "arrive" until we do. Until we are "present" in our "lighter" state, we will never really ascend to any higher ground. Until then, we are off center, banishing the good that waits to come to us, blocking the road to our own miracles with fear and pain, not really capable of accepting joy because our hands are already full. We must empty them. Let go of all we are holding, like angels, trusting that our lives will be filled with diviner things.

❖

When you express your angelic wishes and let your angel do the work, people will go out of their way for you without knowing why. The trick is, you have to back your angel 100%, then the universe backs you.

❖

Angels embody light. They can spread it like honey, express it through words and feelings, shower the world with its Magic, and watch its results—more love, more light, more happiness.

❖

Angels embody wisdom. They accept what is magical and real underlying all experience, so it accepts them and happens all around them.

❖

On a clear night Magic erupts from the soul of an angel like rage from the wicked, causing the air around him to shimmer with wonder, enlivening the atmosphere for miracles, vibrating with the unlimited potential of Heaven, waiting for one pure thought to make a dream come true.

❖

❖ All experiences of Truth are little resurrections of the Spirit. They are the miracles which set us free.

❖ We always know when we have finally stepped out of the way. Because the light pours in.

❖ Our senses never believe in miracles, only our spirits do.

❖ In the middle of any storm there is an eye. In the middle of any miracle there is an "I."

XIX

Trust

Angels are like lighthouses for those passing by in storms.

Divine justice manifests as miracles to the faithful and those brave enough to let go in the dark, to reach for a Greater Hand.

❖

In the darkness we become children—panicky, primal, possessive. In the light we become children of the angels—open flowers reaching for the sun.

❖

This is the essence of angels—to hold on to us in our darkness and befriend us in our light.

❖

An angel has no walls, no defenses, no barriers. He is so naked, he has only light for a body. He is so unshackled, he floats. He is so uninhibited, he sings the music of his soul right out loud.

❖

In the presence of angels our souls become alive again. We grieve no more, we fear no more. We transcend ourselves and become creatures of light without bodies, without minds. We are Spirit and Spirit is us.

❖

We do not cry or struggle but become as One Presence. We fight only the dark veils of our own doubt until we let them all go, and then we really live.

❖

❖ Faith is a messenger of hope that laughs in the face of thieves.

❖ Faith outlives the mighty, undoes the enemy, sweetens the brave.

❖ Faith takes chances on what some cannot see and others cannot imagine, and wins.

❖ Faith exalts life by accepting all its miracles.

❖ Faith rides on unseen wings into the heart of all truly beautiful experiences.

❖ Faith is not a judgment nor an amusement, but a humble acceptance of possibilities.

❖ In the light of faith all shadows dissolve.

❖

Angels move through disturbances in perfect Peace and clarity, always at the eye of the storm, always calm, though the rest of creation rages round them.

Salvation is the sanctuary of safety given as a gift when we are led, like angels, by our fearlessness.

As angels, we empty ourselves into the greater vessel which has no walls . . . diving willingly, knowingly into the unknown . . . forgoing form . . . forgiving all promises . . . releasing function.

❖Move through the world like an angel, holding nothing, feeling everything is a part of you.

❖

As mortals, we avert our eyes from the purity of our souls because they are blinding with Truth, Goodness, and Happiness. We fear we will be swept into the current of Love. And we will.

❖

In the absence of our own inner angels, we find ourselves betrayed by our own doubts, assailed by our own fears and mistrust. But when they are here with us, we are glad for their presence and fear no more.

❖

The Pessimist: I am married to the end of Time because I was born.

The Optimist: I am married to Eternity because I do not make myself afraid.

❖

❖There is Someone watching you always . . . with you always . . . loving you always . . . no matter where you are.

❖In faithlessness we cannot see the ships of love that pass by us in the night.

❖Faith reaches down to where we cannot see and finds us as

little children in the dark, reassuring us that everything will be all right, and quietly turns on the light.

❖In faithlessness we are alone, but the faithful are always accompanied by angels.

❖

Know they protect you; that the angels surround you in times of danger; that your will is their will.

❖

In your thoughts of safety they will guard you; in your feelings of love they will love you; in Peace they will walk with you; and in your freedom they fly with you.

❖

When you express your light, your angels illuminate you. In your wisdom they speak to you. In your courage they stand behind you holding stars of victory over your head. In your humility they will serve all through you. In your ecstasy they will merge inside your heart and shine through you.

❖

It is your purity of intention alone, the deepest sincerity of the heart that must lead you. That is your angel and belongs to God already as a piece of Himself and has a place in Heaven by its very existence.

As angels in life, when we step up to bat, the bat is provided by unseen hands, the ball is pitched by the Cosmic Pitcher, and the angels guide our swing. We revel in the feeling. As people, if we never step up to the plate, we don't play. As mortals, if we sit in the bleachers and don't bother to open our eyes to watch, we never even see the game. We don't even believe it exists. Still, when we are aligned with the Cosmic Team Owner and Umpire, fears do not control the outcome of our game. We are on a special team. A team of angels. Every ball is a home run. Angels always win. There is no better game in town.

❖

❖Faith is like a balloon that carries us to our dreams. Hold its string and sail.

❖Faith holds firm in the face of destructiveness and manipulation.

❖Faith is clarity, not vague hope.

❖Have faith in the Divine and see the world through God's eyes.

❖We *must* trust *someone*. Why not angels?

❖The depth of one's letting go determines the depth of one's freedom.

❖

It is far more dangerous to an angel to be flightless than to fall.

❖

As aspiring angels our Spirits rise teetering in the balanced, freer air of our own souls—not needing to weigh and predict our futures against our pasts; feeling the thrill of weightless surrender to the light and what lies beyond our thoughts; jumping one more time into what was once "the void" but is now recognized as Heaven itself.

❖

❖Faith arranges our lives on invisible calendars and always keeps its appointments.

❖Success in flying comes when we take the weights off ourselves.

❖

I dance up there with you, my angels, tripping on clouds grey blue, in a pale sky, golden light singing by the island of my dreams close by.

❖

My Friends are with me, surrounding my heart with hands of love, molding my destiny, using angel wings to push me gently toward myself.

❖

Sometimes, in thinking too much about the Divine, we have

moved away from Him. To experience someone we do not need too many thoughts. It is not necessary to control our experience of Heaven or seek specific answers all the time. It is the right way just to be with Him.

PART FOUR

—

BEYOND

—

ANGEL DREAMS

XX

Peace

———

Peace is the quiet place under the mighty Wing of God.

Peace is not an achievement to be reached, a prize to be strived for nor a commodity to be gained. Peace is a condition of Spirit —a part of that which we are, existing in everything; like the bones of the universe.

❖

Peace is not a vessel to be filled with different experiences. It is a magical pool of Truth and Love that shines all around us and inside us silently every day.

❖

❖ Peace is the seed of eternity from which quietness the tree of life grows.

❖ Peace fulfills all righteousness as a dove fulfills flight.

❖ Peace answers the question "Who am I?" with the answer, "I Am."

❖ Peace rules from the throne of goodwill at the heart of all beings waiting for its subjects to volunteer.

❖ Peace dissolves the walls we build to hide from ourselves.

❖ Peace sweeps away the dust stirred up by all the other motions of the soul.

❖

In Peace, Time stops without comment. There is no rush to solve the crimes of our hearts or mend what is broken. In Peace, we rejoice in the healing and Time stands still. In Peace, our lives are washed clean in the pure light that emerges from our surrendered selves.

❖

In Peace there is no dark, no light, no sorrow, only Life unending, ageless and whole.

❖

❖ Peace, like Home, is where you find it.

❖ Peace appears suddenly where it has always been, like the sun.

❖ There are many roads to Peace, but only one direction.

❖

Peace is a land with no boundaries or borders, no entrance or exit, no signs to tell you where you are or where you're going, but it feels wonderful to be there.

❖

- ❖In Peace all is still, yet never stuck.

- ❖Peace is Harmony, yet soundless.

- ❖Peace is a poem in the hands of a child that says everything without words.

- ❖Peace is the simple Truth that everything boils down to.

- ❖Peace doesn't care if or when you arrive because you are already there without knowing it.

- ❖Peace is present everywhere yet rules from a throne at the heart of all Beings.

- ❖Graceful is the one who knows the path of Peace and walks it.

❖

Out of the hands of the mighty come pebbles of Truth. But one grain of Wisdom from the peacemaker is like a mountain that all may use as a lookout.

❖

- ❖Out of the ashes of the Peacemakers come the seeds of inspiration.

- ❖Peace is without ambition, yet possesses all things.

❖The Peaceful have always been the most powerful upon the earth, for it is in them that both weak and strong find refuge from their cares.

❖Peace is a perfect mirror of unlimited potential.

❖Peace is everlasting—like God.

❖

All voices become silent in the greater resonance of Peace, which rings endlessly beyond all thinking.

❖

Peace is a river running silently behind closed eyes when our Consciousness is in repose, focused on Truth, Oneness, Perfection.

❖

Set upon the road to Heaven, the one that passes right through your own heart into the depths of your most glorious soul, where even God whispers because all is so delightful even He wouldn't disturb it.

❖

❖There is no singing in Peace . . . for it is where the angels go to rest from their joy.

❖

If we were to ignore all our feelings, we would not find Peace. If

126

we were to chase our desires to their ends, we would not find Peace. If we were to find our truest loves and define ourselves by them, we would not find Peace. For Peace is past these strivings. Peace is past ownership. Peace is past any manipulation. Peace lives beyond the point of earthly happiness. It is the very fabric of the Great Beyond that exists within us all.

❖

❖Peace wavers on the edge of our Consciousness until we fall in.

❖Peace is not merely an absence of war.

❖To the soul and heart, Peace is a rich, full, boundless experience of Completeness, Oneness, Trust and All Knowing.

❖Peace is rainfall to the thirsty, an island to those lost at sea.

❖

Peace is all that is invisible yet speaks and dances and shines behind our thoughts.

❖

❖There is no price for Peace. It does not cost us anything, and it cannot be bought.

❖Peace lives complete unto itself, yet One with all.

❖Peace cannot be forged, imitated, or counterfeited.

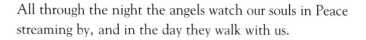

❖

All through the night the angels watch our souls in Peace
streaming by, and in the day they walk with us.

❖

Peace is a guiding element, a structural constant of the
universe, a never broken line. It threads through us, our
bodies, our lives, invisibly; through our cells, through the air,
through plants and rocks and all things. It is the basic
expression of all that is, upon which all things move and grow,
from whence all expression emerges.

❖

Only to the man of Peace does reality seem consistent. To the
degree we identify with our own sense of Peace, life will behave
peacefully toward us. We will see and feel Peace wherever
we go.

❖

Peace is not a gift given to the winner in life, it is a timeless
tribute to the core of our Being. It is the nature of our souls. It
is a perfect, poised experience of who we are. Peace is the
absence of turmoil, the fruition of spiritual goals.

❖

❖Peace is invisible but contains all colors like light.

❖Peace is the child under a tree waiting for no one, asking nothing, yet receiving Everything.

❖Peace is an answered prayer.

❖Peace is the soldier who never has to fight.

❖Peace is not frightened by anything.

❖Peace has no problems. It is the solution.

❖Peace is God's vibration.

❖Peace rules the gates of Heaven with one quiet hand on the latch to let some come in and others go.

❖Peace enjoins the saint to pray, the leaf to fall, the baby to slumber.

❖Peace sings no song aloud. It prefers the subtler music of silence.

❖Peace finds its own level, like water.

❖Peace comes to the mighty when they have forfeited their might for Freedom.

❖

Peace finds Magic in the light . . . a symphony in the darkness . . . simplicity in an empire . . . and birth among the dead.

❖

Nothing compares to the Peace of the soul because it is the only experience that satisfies human nature, completely.

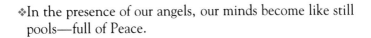

❖In the presence of our angels, our minds become like still
pools—full of Peace.

❖

The feeling of Peace will pervade our lives as soon as we are
attracted to the Real more than the unreal.

❖

In the quiet of the night the angels gather around us silently
wishing us Peace because it is often the only time we will
accept any.

❖

Peace is that which exists at the bottom of all layers of
confusion. It is at the beginning of our minds, at the source of
the soul. The universe has perfect patience, perfect power,
perfect poise.

❖

It is not difficult to find. Peace is where it has always been.
Peace will never be found outside until it is known inwardly.
For there is no other measure for Peace but Peace. And there is
only one Peace, and it is uniform and universal.

❖

Stillness gives birth to us and accepts all the noise we bring to it, yet remains unchanged.

❖

❖Peace is a kettle of water that always boils but never whistles.

❖Peace conquers its enemies, not with force, but by their undoing.

❖Peace makes all things peaceful in its path.

❖When whole nations bend to serve the wishes of one gentle soul, it is because they have heard the peaceful voice of an angel.

❖One glimpse of our true angel nature would give us more Peace than a thousand peeks into the future.

❖Peace does not desire to change the world, for in Peace, all is well and ever was and will be.

XXI

Communion

When we commune as angels with all Life, we see everything in the light of our joy.

As aspiring angels, we flow like rivers, around, over, and through obstacles. We float like birds, supported, watchful, free to choose our own direction. We pour love effortlessly through all the cracks and crevices of our existence like light. We are awake, unbound, radiant.

❖

In communion with angels, we experience the most Heavenly qualities, the holiest, noblest, selfless ambitions, complete with unending power to achieve them—true soul-sprung values and morals, acceptance and wisdom, toward all.

❖

❖All our troubles cease the minute we merge with the Source of all solutions.

❖ As angels, waiting in the silence, we are full of song. Waiting in the shadows, we are filled with light.

❖ The presences of all angels come together within my soul—and grow and grow until I am one of them.

❖ No one and nothing in the universe resists an angel . . . because an angel holds no resistance.

❖

It is not the angels' job to baby us, but our job to grow up, and to join them.

❖

Where truth is spoken and understood, the angels stop to pay respects and listen. They know there are angels being born.

❖

When communing with your angels, sing: "I am the earth to your sky. I am the wind to your rain. I am all the seasons when you are Time. I live in your Harmony."

❖

As angels, we are led by the heart to the greatest heart of all—the heart within all hearts, beating soundlessly like wings of angels across the vast landscapes of our unencumbered Being.

XXII

Love

As angels, love is the light we see by.

The power of love is the key to every idiosyncrasy in creation.
It melts the gates of ignorance, tramples the barbed wire of
anger and grinds it into fairy dust.

❖

It is the tidings of all good souls that hold together this universe
—loving thoughts bathe and caress us with Peace and infuse us
with light. All souls know one another through the fabric of
Love.

❖

❖ Love is the strength that shines through our weakness; the
vision in our blindness. It is pure, whole, and perfect, shining
through Everything.

❖ In Love we will see ourselves for what we are. Without our
judgments.

As angels we remove the layers and see the seed of Love, peel away the wrapper and see the structure of Love, wipe away the dirt and see through the window of Love.

❖

We will stand free in the soil of creation—light, growing, unimpeded. We'll release all considerations about Truth and know the source of our own Love.

❖

As angels, we must find our wings here on earth, if we are ever to know our angels . . . and to know our own imperturbable Being where nothing and no one can ever disturb us again.

❖

The immortal roots of Love grow deep. They cannot be cut or burned by force or deception, but drink at the spring of Eternity and never fade or rot though the earth itself blow away to dust.

❖

Love is never squeamish, shy, or humiliated by circumstances. It is sometimes outspoken and bold, outrageous and laughing, or subtle and tender, tenacious and filled with compassion.

❖

❖Love always gets what it wants and always gives all it has.

❖Love stops no one in their tracks but may change the very course of the street on which we are walking.

❖When we say "Love is my reason for being," we have joined the league of the angels.

❖

It does not matter if we approach Love bravely like a lion or delicately like a little flower . . . powerfully like an elephant or gracefully like a butterfly—so long as we approach.

❖

Dwell upon happy, positive feelings. Follow them to their source within you. There, you will find an angel promoting your freedom and encouraging your participation in this Divine quest for Love.

❖

See your angel-self reflected all the time in the mirror of everything. It is not dependent on what the body is doing or the circumstances surrounding it. None of that even reflects. Only the light.

❖

❖Angels are eternal. They have an inexhaustible supply of Love.

❖As angels, the winds of Love move through us effortlessly.

❖

Angels are not only empty of darkness, but full of light; not empty of hate, but filled with love; not empty of misery, but full of joy.

❖

As mortals, we are loving dreams, worshiping dreams, until as angels we know the reality that is not a dream beyond all our little dreams.

❖

❖ Through the angelic presence of Love our lives become worthwhile.

❖ When minds sail out of Heaven's way the flutes of Love begin to play.

❖

As angels, we are miracle workers, Heavenly-charged souls, glowing with the fires of Truth and Love to warm each other on cold days.

❖

It is better to let the heart break than hold off that which would break it using all one's might—because then there is no strength left to love with. And a broken heart may be reborn— but a heart engaged thus in battle cannot die nor live nor love at all.

❖

❖Love is a pure drink to those thirsting for meaning.

❖There is nothing greater than the desire to love, except love itself.

❖Our angels are there with us when we fall in love, when something beautiful makes us cry.

❖Love says, "If you touch me, I will take your hand and we will rise together."

❖

He who approaches Heaven correctly is protected. It doesn't take special strength or intelligence. It is your purity of intention alone, the deepest sincerity of the heart that must lead you. That is your angel who belongs to God already as a piece of Himself, and has a place in Heaven by its very existence.

❖

In the middle of all the chaos and confusion there is light. There is hope. There are miracles of Love happening right in the middle of our despair. There are flowers blooming in the arid deserts of human hearts.

❖

❖Angels fly, transcending every barrier to Love.

❖Love gives freely to each weary person who needs respite from their woes.

❖

Often We ask of another, "Do you love me?" If we listen, the angels always answer, "Does the sky love the moon? Our Love surrounds you. Rise or set . . . We are here."

❖

Angels' voices are speaking to us always. In the silence of our Love, the angels whisper, "Rest, O little ones. Feel Peace. Come home. We are awaiting you with open arms. Our Love will heal you—we know what you need. Come in to our circle of Love and be rejuvenated. The world's tortures will fall off you like shackles dropping." The angels sing, "We will take you in our arms, again, you whom we love most preciously. You have returned to us and we are glad."

❖

They comfort us, "There is great Love for you. There is great light awaiting you and also within you. Your Heavenly friends are deeply moved by your earnest seeking and loyalty. As guardians we will caress your soul, tenderly and with great joy. Our patience is limitless. We know nothing but love. We love you."

XXIII

Being

*Becoming an angel is to transcend our own limits, to unbury the
Truth of all things, and to be swept into Perfection.*

Because it has no words, it does not speak. And because there
are no words for it, we rarely speak of it.

❖

Our Being is a wonder that has no name, no sound, no bells
that ring, no books written about it, no movies whose images
capture it—no earthly treasures that compare to owning it.

❖

Our unlimited Being is beyond our traveling to it—beyond the
boat that gets us there, the distance we have come and the
person who arrives.

❖

When we move toward the center of our Being, we find all

As people, we sometimes get stuck in our roles, overdesigning and trying to perfect them when they're really only passing thoughts—passing shadows in our dream. Life seems confusing and out of control because we're not consciously living it. We are asleep thinking we're awake.

❖

It is what we feel if we had let go of our worldly identity, our emotional wardrobe. Your inner angel doesn't need to be defined by any limiting facts. It lives beyond statistics, beyond our labels and plans, beyond the right and wrong of things, beyond all opposites. It is just pure Being.

❖

As angels, when we awaken, the lights go on . . . the fog clears . . . all the shadows and nightmares vanish. We remember who we are; we find the freedom to choose any role, the clarity to see where Home really is, and the will and desire to go there—to be who we are like angels. We wake up in our own beds, we hear the birds singing in our souls, and it is sweet, very sweet, to be here.

❖

For there is only one experience that will really free us; that we build our lives for; that we sacrifice and plan for; that we cherish in our secret fantasies with our eyes closed in our beds

—that is the full-blown wonder of who and what we are, our own angelic selves, our own unlimited Beingness.

❖

The angels tell us it is all right here. There is nowhere else to look. Our eyes must see to the core of our own Being or we will be blind all our lives and will have seen nothing.

❖

The angels long for us to know them. They do not see our imaginings. They see only the Truth, which never changes because they are a part of it.

❖

If tranquillity comes from knowing all is well, where does our "knowing" come from? Only when we experience our innate tranquillity do we become knowing people. Similarly, when we experience Peace within ourselves, like the angels, our lives will change to reflect it.

❖

It is only remembering what we truly are which keeps us sane, and loving which keeps us whole.

❖

With each release of pretense, we gain conviction about who we are. There is no other way to truly find ourselves.

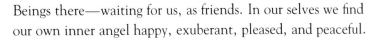

Beings there—waiting for us, as friends. In our selves we find our own inner angel happy, exuberant, pleased, and peaceful.

❖

We see the colors and Beauty of nature from within her. We know the heart of life because we are there inside its loving chambers. We see more clearly because the walls become thinner, transparent, as we move toward the source of ourselves. Shadows become fewer, light and dark become more transparent, and the clear joy of Being which radiates from the One becomes air, food, motive, vision.

❖

There is less thinking, more knowing; less to do, more potential—less to be, more Being. Nothing lacking; there is no time; all awareness; there is no fighting; just equanimity. There is no possession, only having; there is no pressure, resistance, or regret, just effortlessness, ease, and Peace.

❖

The real substance of our Being is unaffected by our struggles. It is effervescent, pure, and all knowing; never leaning on technique or process; never asking for reasons, but full of cause; existing eternally, always in full bloom, in perfect voice, attached to the thread of Harmony—always . . . like an angel.

❖

❖

It has been said that "the Truth is that which never changes."
If there is any Truth to us, it is that ultimate unchanging Being
of which we are all a part.

❖

Before we could think, we Were. When we stop thinking, we
will Be, still.

❖

As human beings we are all the time attempting the impossible;
trying to make reality out of unreality; trying to capture that
which we can only Be. Aching and striving to become what we
already are; seeking that which we always were, will always be,
can never not be.

❖

As angels we may walk the edge of the sword of our own
achievements, because then we are the masters and not the
victims of ourselves. Then Peace is our crown and our Glory, and
we are remarkable because unafraid. For life does not glorify
itself nor serve any hidden masters, and neither should we.

❖

As angels we can simply Be here, taking life from the Divine
well from which we spring, and because we are human, keep

removing layers that block us from our real, essential nature which is behind it all.

❖

As human beings our greatest option is to escape into our unlimited Being . . . to free ourselves from all self-imposed prisons . . . to return to full Harmony with Nature, God, each other, ourselves . . . to reveal for ourselves our innate soul Wisdom.

❖

❖As angels, we may discover Heaven within our own Being, and walk with it wherever we go.

XXIV

Summary

We are all sometimes as angels in the dark. Therefore, we must hold our vision high and believe in the Beauty and Magic of the Light. We should not feel alone because there are others who will join us from distant lands and foreign places and always from Above. And one day, we will all join hands and the miracle will be the Light that shines on everyone.

❖

Stay in contact with angels and your life will become dreamlike, ushering in all the good you ever dreamed possible, deeply nourishing all your truest loves, finding Peace and grace supremely, feeling cared for and guarded and guided through Eternity.

❖

Live like a window in Consciousness, letting all good pass through you; letting all Love pass in and out of your own heart. Let Happiness flow everywhere. Be a part of the Light. Love and release the darkness. Heal all by healing yourself.

❖

Follow your own star as a sign. It waits for you. Your angel will illuminate many lives. Never doubt that the way will be set and the path cleared when the miracle of light is brought forth from the darkness inside you. Outside you will shine, while inside you will relax like a child in a garden nestled safely in the bosom of your angels, and all will be Light.

❖

❖Allow the windows of your soul to open to the fresh air of God.

❖

Hear the angels singing: "Our care is your care. Our passion is your passion. Our heart is your heart. We are with you in your light and your darkness. We stand by you in your unhappiness and your joy. We live in your presence because you live in ours."

❖

In this life, remember, you are an angel. Your diary is full of angel experiences already.

❖

Confront the trials that beset you now and then with an open heart.

❖

Learn what real love is. Keep an open heart—that's your work now.

❖

Never worry. Be joyful. Be happy. Be light. Stop hiding from your happy self.

❖

Live in Peace, for in Peace you will find all that you do not find elsewhere.

❖

Know that others must never be oppressed, but that all should rise up to Love. Accept that all *must* return on the same inner route.

❖

Begin with yourself. Begin to be an angel *for* you and then with the people around you. Begin now.

❖

To be an angel, you must bring all parts of yourself Home . . . the broken and the fearful . . . the shining and the brave. All parts know Home as Freedom where everything will be made right again. One day, one hour, when you are ready, when

Peace becomes priority, when Freedom becomes utterly necessary to your existence, when you know deep inside there is no time left to fantasize, when you need to heal more than hurt—in that hour, you are Home forever.

❖

Be patient with yourself. Your own inner angel has been patiently waiting for you to recognize her all your life.

❖

Release more, love more, trust more, seek answers more, find more of yourself. Don't be afraid of deep Peace. It will enliven everything you do, everything you think, everything you say. One day you will be only That.

❖

Be all that you Are. Be That. Release all thoughts of limitation. Live like an abundant and free king or queen of the universe. Tell others how.

❖

Always believe in the power of Heaven that exists in and beyond Creation.

❖

What we need more than anything are the angelic messengers of our own wisdom, teaching us the power of Unity.

❖

It is our angels' voices we will hear when our thoughts are empty and our hearts are full.

❖

As advanced aspiring angels, affirm: "We are ready for the Light, finished with being afraid; no longer do we believe in 'impossibilities' or in the glory of 'things.' "

❖

Ask your angels to stay as near you as they can; to help keep your vision clear and your presence simple, so in all the days to come there will be a radiance and Glory in your spirit.

❖

Remember, as a mortal, you are holding on to your own limitations, as angel you can let them go.

❖

Know that you can let go within and join your angels, orchestrating all the Love present in everything noble and worthy and kind.

❖

Know you embody within you the miracle of undying Truth, the infinite power of the way Home, and the answers to all questions.

Trust that in the sanctity of your innermost Being, beyond your deepest fears, beyond your broken heart, beyond your brilliant mind, you can know and feel as angels feel—can grow toward Eternity—will dare to fly.

❖

Know that the angels want to give you back all the lost pieces of yourself, to tell you you are not alone, not forgotten; that you can be Free by finding the reality of the Heaven within yourself.

❖

Go into the world with the wind of love in your hair and Peace on your lips and tell many people what you know in your heart. And when they ask you how you know such Freedom, tell them it came to you from the depths of your soul—from your heart, and your angels.

❖

As angels—we can play any role in life successfully, wear any costume, accomplish any goal we choose. But now we will know which is the reality and which is only a game.

❖

As angels, wherever you go hearts will smile, angels will awaken. In humility, yet united with all things, you will know the Freedom the angels know. The greatest forces in the universe will unite behind you to carry you to your goals.

❖

As an aspiring angel, you will be given the right words to speak with, a healed heart to love with and a deep sense of your own Truth.

ASPIRING ANGEL
INSTRUCTIONS

———

*I*t takes courage and will to do the right thing. To act in Harmony with all men's greater good and therefore to think properly and see clearly.

❖

If there were a ship floundering, wouldn't you rescue it if you could? Of course. But do we ever rescue ourselves? Hardly ever.

❖

Stop looking for people who can answer all your questions for you and lead you through life. People are only human. Count on your angels for the miracles you require and seek their loving voices.

❖

Let go of resisting what your angel wants to do—it only wants to love, to free you to do the greatest things. It wants to resolve your conflicts, ease worries, clear confusion, discover the way to your own Peace.

❖

Angels help you reclaim your real self and your deepest innermost thoughts and Being. What defines you can never be found on the surface of life. Look deep inside yourself for what you need to the perfect, beautiful, heavenly, adorable, interested, caring, innocent, giving, most wonderful part of you —your inner angel.

❖

Remember, it doesn't need fanfare. It is your own inner angel, humble yet utterly profound, waiting to be claimed by you.

❖

Keep a journal of your angelic thoughts. Let your soul speak to you in language you've never heard before. One day it will speak through you to everyone.

❖

When you let your inner angel show, you help millions. You remind everyone of the standard of living in Heaven. *You* are the message. They see something special in you. It goes in past their personality, slides into their souls through the back door, silently. . . . Then, it will knock from within and speak to them.

❖

Express what it is to be an angel. Be happy. Be free.

❖

Pledge your love and devotion to the angel inside you and it becomes "yours" forever. It will never leave you. You'll find you have the strength of thousands, love enough for millions.

❖

Be true to your inner angel and all angels will be true to you.

❖

Ask them to shine their light on you so that you may see more clearly.

❖

Within a Human Being is the seed of the Universe; the signature of God's power and love and wisdom; the collective voice of the angels; the presence and purpose and potential of life; and the history and future of all creatures, all men, all beings.

❖

❖Accept your angels' blessings and light and worry no more.

AN ANGEL PROMISE

---

*I*n your feeling of well-being you will hear them rejoicing, "There is nowhere you can go that we cannot find you; nowhere to hide that we cannot see you, nothing you can feel that we will not love you. In your asleepness you see dangers and monsters and pain, but when you awaken you are free again. We will help you find the Happiness that does not rust or decay, but shines like a million suns and never goes away."

If you've had an "angel experience"—
feeling, vision, or encounter—
we'd like to hear about it or
anything else you'd like to share
about how you relate to angels.

Please send your story or thoughts to:

Karen Goldman
8721 Santa Monica Blvd. #118
West Hollywood, CA 90069–4511